Medieval World

Medieval Warfare

Tara Steele

 Crabtree Publishing Company

www.crabtreebooks.com

Crabtree Publishing Company

www.crabtreebooks.com

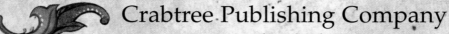

PMB 16A, 350 Fifth Avenue
Suite 3308
New York, NY 10118

612 Welland Avenue,
St. Catharines,
Ontario, Canada
L2M 5V6

73 Lime Walk
Headington
Oxford 0X3 7AD
United Kingdom

Coordinating editor: Ellen Rodger

Series editor: Carrie Gleason

Design and production coordinator: Rosie Gowsell

Scanning technician: Arlene Arch-Wilson

Art director: Rob MacGregor

Project development, editing, photo editing, and layout: First Folio Resource Group, Inc.: Erinn Banting, Molly Bennett, Tom Dart, Jaimie Nathan, Debbie Smith, Anikó Szöcs

Photo research: Maria DeCambra

Prepress: Embassy Graphics

Printing: Worzalla Publishing Company

Consultants: Joseph Goering, Department of History, University of Toronto; Linda Northrup, Department of Near and Middle Eastern Civilizations, University of Toronto; David Waterhouse, Professor Emeritus of East Asian Studies, University of Toronto

Photographs: Paul Almasy/Corbis/Magma: p. 16; Archives Charmet/Bridgeman Art Library: p. 9 (top); Archivo Iconografico, S.A./Corbis/Magma: title page, p. 4, p. 5 (top); Art Archive/Biblioteca Augusta Perugia/Dagli Orti: p. 30; Art Archive/Biblioteca Nazionale Marciana Venice/Dagli Orti: p. 6; Art Archive/Bibliothèque des Arts Décoratifs Paris/Harper Collins Publishers: p. 17 (top); Art Archive/Mireille Vautier: p. 31 (right); Bibliothèque Nationale, France/Français 2644 f. 135: p. 18; British Library, London, UK/Bridgeman Art Library: p. 31 (left); British Library/Royal 20 C. VII f.34: p. 25; British Library/Topham-HIP/The Image Works: p. 9 (bottom); Burstein Collection/Corbis/Magma: p. 11; Mary Evans Picture Library: p. 8 (left), p. 22, p. 24, p. 27 (top right);

Werner Forman/Art Resource, NY: p. 12 (bottom); Giraudon/Art Resource, NY: p. 13 (bottom); Erich Lessing/Art Resource, NY: p. 7 (bottom); North Wind Picture Archives: p. 8 (right), p. 15 (top), p. 23 (bottom right); Réunion des Musées Nationaux/Art Resource, NY: p. 29 (bottom); Rougemont Maurice/Corbis Sygma/Magma: p. 15 (bottom); Royalty-Free/Corbis/Magma: p. 17 (bottom); Snark/Art Resource, NY: p. 13 (top); Chase Swift/Corbis/Magma: pp. 26–27

Illustrations: Jeff Crosby: pp. 20–21; Katherine Kantor: flags, title page (border), p. 9 (box), p. 23 (top left, middle right, middle left); Margaret Amy Reiach: border, gold boxes, title page (illuminated letter), copyright page, contents page (all), pp. 4-5 (timeline), p. 5 (map), p. 7 (top), p. 10 (both), p. 12 (top), p.14. p. 19 (top and bottom), p. 28 (map), p. 29 (top), p. 32 (all)

Cover: This illustration from the 1400s shows a castle in France under siege. This siege lasted for six months!

Title page: Attackers used a type of catapult called a trebuchet to hurl rocks at castle residents. Then, the residents dropped the rocks back on the attackers.

Published by
Crabtree Publishing Company

Cataloging-in-Publication Data
Steele, Tara.
 Medieval warfare / written by Tara Steele.
  p. cm. -- (Medieval world series)
Includes index.
Contents: The Middle Ages -- A noble's land -- Knights -- Raids -- The Vikings -- Castles -- Keeping safe -- Under attack -- Siege! -- Warriors and their weapons -- On the battlefield -- In the name of god -- The Crusades -- A new age begins.
 ISBN 0-7787-1344-X (RLB) -- ISBN 0-7787-1376-8 (pbk)
 1. Military art and science--History--Medieval, 500-1500--Juvenile literature.
2. Military history, Medieval--Juvenile literature. [1. Military art and science--History--Medieval, 500-1500. 2. Military history, Medieval.] I. Title. II. Series.
 U37.S74 2003
  355'.0094'0902--dc22
                    2003016189
                    LC

Table of Contents

The Middle Ages

For hundreds of years, the enormous stretch of land from England to Egypt was known as the Roman Empire. The empire's **powerful government built roads and well-organized towns that had plumbing, sewers, dams, and** aqueducts.

The Roman Empire fell apart after 410 A.D. when tribes of German warriors attacked Rome. These warriors, called barbarians by the Romans, killed innocent people, stole what they needed, and set fire to everything else.

After the fall of the Roman Empire, western Europe was divided into smaller **kingdoms**, which fought each other over land. For the next thousand years, from about 500 A.D. to 1500 A.D., fighting became a way of life. This period is known as the Middle Ages.

▲ *Knights were warriors who fought on horseback, using swords and lances to defeat their enemies.*

Roman Empire
collapses

410 A.D.

First Viking
attacks on Britain

793

Battle of Hastings

1066

Siege of Antioch

1098

700s
Stirrups, which come
from China, are used
throughout Europe

1000s
Knights begin
wearing chain mail

1095
Pope Urban II's speech
triggers crusades

Attacks from near and far

During the Middle Ages, Viking **invaders** from what is now Denmark and Norway **raided** villages in Europe. Large armies clashed on battlefields. **Nobles**, such as kings, barons, and lords, attacked castles where other nobles lived, sometimes fighting for months until the defenders starved to death or gave up.

▲ *Soldiers during the Middle Ages carried shields to protect themselves from arrows and spears.*

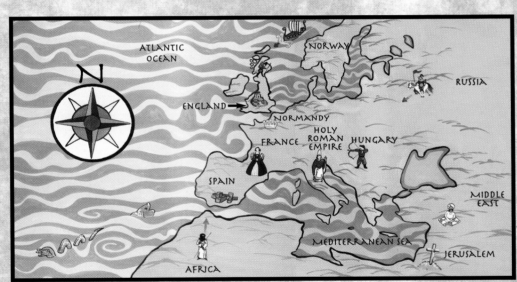

1100s
Siege engines widely used

1150
Stone curtain walls and towers added to castles

1206
Genghis Khan organizes Mongol tribes into one army

1270
Last main crusade begins

1300s
Gunpowder used in battle

1337
Beginning of Hundred Years War between France and England

1400s
Knights and horses wear full suits of plate armor

A Noble's Land

Most of western Europe was divided into areas of land ruled by kings. The more land kings owned, the more powerful they were.

A king gave other nobles parts of his land to manage and protect for him. The nobles, who were called vassals, made laws, were judges in courts, and collected taxes from the peasants who farmed the land.

In exchange for this power, each vassal promised to be loyal to the king, to fight in the king's army, and to provide knights in times of war. This system of receiving land in exchange for military service is called the feudal system, or feudalism.

Nobles with large territories needed help defending their land. They gave sections of land to less wealthy nobles, who became their vassals. Vassals often promised to be loyal to more than one lord, which caused problems if the two lords went to war against each other. Vassals sometimes chose to protect one lord, their liege lord, above all others.

▶ *Kings did not want their nobles to have more power than they did. Some, such as King Stephen of Hungary, gave nobles smaller sections of land scattered around the country, rather than large areas of land.*

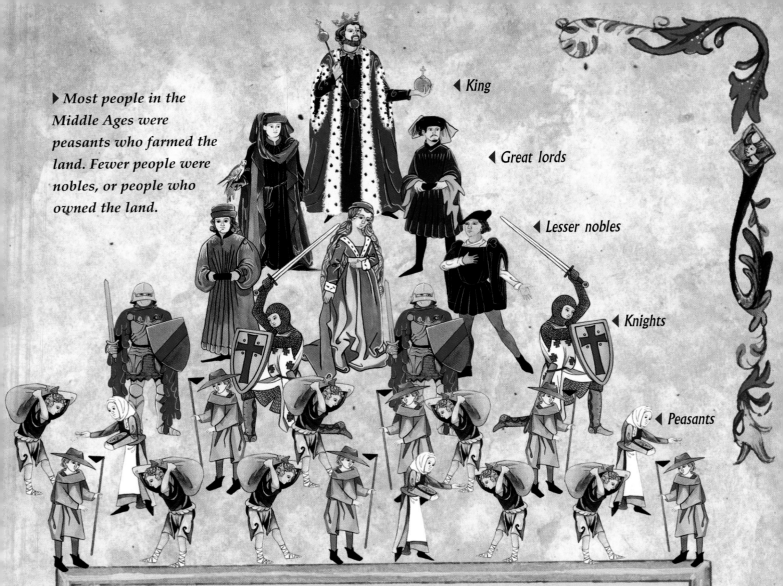

▶ Most people in the Middle Ages were peasants who farmed the land. Fewer people were nobles, or people who owned the land.

◀ King

◀ Great lords

◀ Lesser nobles

◀ Knights

◀ Peasants

Medieval Japan

During the Middle Ages, Japan had a system that was similar to feudalism. Japanese farmers were loyal to powerful landowners, or *daimyo*, who gave them land to farm. In exchange, these farmers fought for the *daimyo*, who were battling one another for control of the countryside. Over time, many farmers became warriors known as samurai.

Knights

Knights were vassals who fought on horseback for their overlords in exchange for land. Some knights lived for part of the year in their lord's castle as part of his permanent guard, or garrison.

▲ *Knights agreed to fight for about 40 days each year. The rest of the year, they watched over their land and practiced their skills in tournaments, which were pretend battles fought before audiences.*

▼ *Knights rode fast, powerful horses, called destriers, that were also covered in armor.*

Becoming a Knight

When the son of a noble was seven years old, he went to live in another lord's castle. The lord was usually his father's liege lord or someone his father wanted as an **ally**. At first, the boy worked as a page. He learned to carve meat, serve meals, and run errands. He was also taught good manners and how to fight with small weapons.

At fourteen years of age, the page became a squire. He learned how to ride a horse, hunt, wrestle, and use large weapons. Most importantly, he cleaned the knight's armor, looked after the knight's horse, and followed the knight into battle. Between the ages of 18 and 21, a squire who had proved his skills became a knight.

Samurai

The Japanese samurai fought on horseback and on foot, and were experts with bows and swords. In the 1600s, they developed a code of honor called *bushido*, or "the way of the warrior." *Bushido* required that samurai live honestly, be loyal to their masters, and die willingly. If samurai failed in any way, they were expected to kill themselves by cutting open their stomachs. This practice was called *seppuku*.

Knights in Armor

Knights dressed to protect themselves from their enemies' swords and arrows. They wore layers of clothing made from linen, wool, leather, and metal. Chain mail, which was made of metal rings hooked together, was used for shirts, leggings, and gloves.

As more powerful weapons were invented, knights needed heavier armor. Solid metal plates were made to cover a knight's chest and back. By the end of the Middle Ages, knights wore whole suits of plate armor. Wealthy knights also covered their destriers in armor made of steel or hardened leather.

▶ *An armorer linked thousands of iron rings together to make a long mail shirt called a hauberk, such as that worn by the knight on the left. The knight on the right wore an early type of plate armor.*

Raids

In the Middle Ages, some warriors traveled great distances searching for land to conquer. These raiders stole food and drink and captured people to hold for ransom or to sell as slaves. Innocent people were forced to give the raiders money or goods in exchange for their lives.

◀ The Magyars

Magyars came from the area north of the Black Sea and settled in Hungary in 889. They spent part of the year farming, hunting, and raising horses for sale. The rest of the year, they raided the area that is now Germany, Italy, and Austria for money, prisoners to sell as slaves, and valuable goods.

Magyars attacked quickly on horseback, shooting arrows at their enemies. They also fought with curved swords and short spears. The Magyars were so dangerous that many rulers paid them to stay away.

The Moors ▶

The Moors were a group of **Muslims** from North Africa who invaded Spain in 711. Within seven years, they captured most of the country from **Christians** who ruled Spain before them. The Moors built schools, hospitals, and palaces decorated with colored tiles, introduced new foods such as dates and oranges, and made Spain a place of learning. After much fighting, Christians regained control of the country in 1492.

The Christians and Moors had very different fighting styles. The Christians rode large warhorses and fought with broad swords. The Moors rode horses that were small and quick, and fought with bows, spears, and curved swords.

▼ The Mongols

The Mongols were nomads who traveled across central Asia looking for grazing land for their animals. In the late 1100s, a chief named Temujin organized the Mongols into a powerful army. Within 20 years, they controlled the largest territory in the world, covering central Asia and most of China. Temujin became known as Genghis Khan, which means "Universal Ruler."

The Mongols fought on horseback and attacked their enemies quickly from all sides. Standing in their stirrups, they shot six or more arrows every minute. Other favorite weapons were curved swords and halberds. Halberds were wooden poles with long blades that could slice through the legs of an enemy's horse. Mongol warriors wore metal helmets with leather flaps and long leather coats covered in rectangular metal plates to protect themselves from their enemies' weapons.

The Vikings

At the end of the 700s, small tribes of Vikings from northern Europe began to invade neighboring lands. Some Vikings were looking for farmland. Others were hoping to trade furs, wood, and slaves for weapons, silver, and spices.

Viking Longboats

Vikings traveled in wooden boats, called longboats, which held between 20 and 100 people. The front of the boat was often carved in the shape of an animal, such as a serpent. On the side of the boat was a rack called a batten, which held the warriors' shields as they traveled. The boats' sails were dyed red, the color of blood. In bad weather, the sail was used as a tent to protect the warriors.

Longboats were strong enough to sail over the ocean, but they could also be rowed in very shallow water. This meant Vikings traveled quietly up rivers, attacked their enemies by surprise, and quickly escaped.

▼ *When Viking rulers died, they were placed in longboats that were then buried. This oak warship, which was found buried in Oseberg, Norway, was built around 800 A.D.*

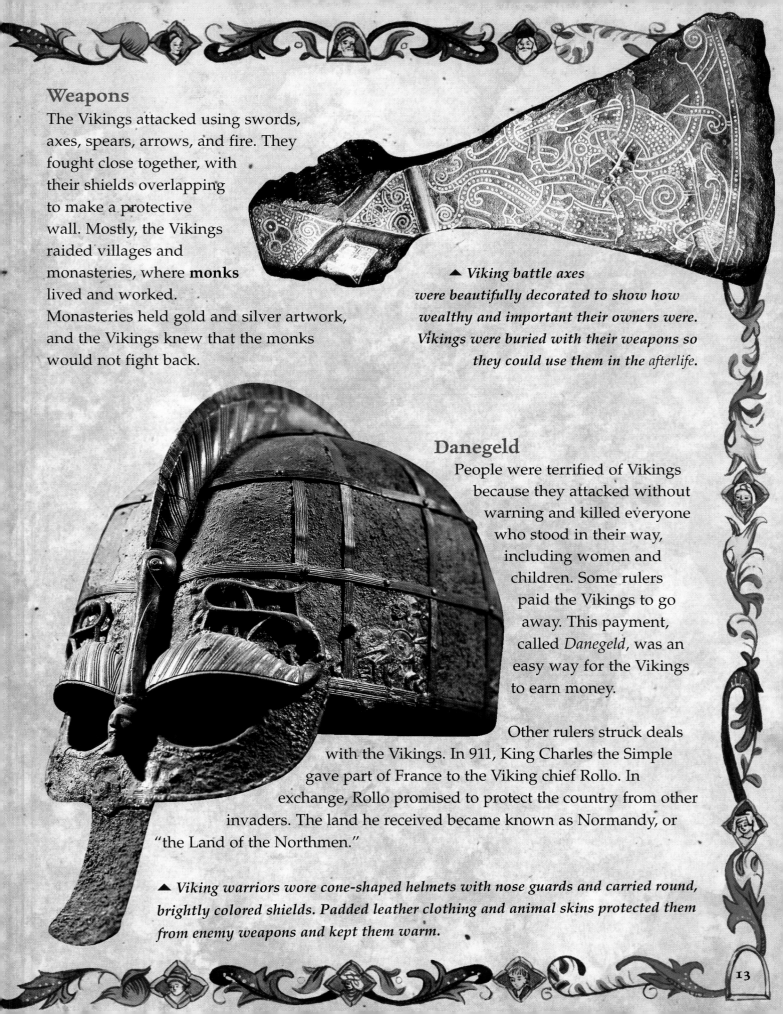

Weapons

The Vikings attacked using swords, axes, spears, arrows, and fire. They fought close together, with their shields overlapping to make a protective wall. Mostly, the Vikings raided villages and monasteries, where **monks** lived and worked. Monasteries held gold and silver artwork, and the Vikings knew that the monks would not fight back.

▲ *Viking battle axes were beautifully decorated to show how wealthy and important their owners were. Vikings were buried with their weapons so they could use them in the* afterlife.

Danegeld

People were terrified of Vikings because they attacked without warning and killed everyone who stood in their way, including women and children. Some rulers paid the Vikings to go away. This payment, called *Danegeld*, was an easy way for the Vikings to earn money.

Other rulers struck deals with the Vikings. In 911, King Charles the Simple gave part of France to the Viking chief Rollo. In exchange, Rollo promised to protect the country from other invaders. The land he received became known as Normandy, or "the Land of the Northmen."

▲ *Viking warriors wore cone-shaped helmets with nose guards and carried round, brightly colored shields. Padded leather clothing and animal skins protected them from enemy weapons and kept them warm.*

Castles

A castle was home to a noble, his family, and his servants. It was also a symbol of the noble's power, and it protected the noble from invaders.

Nobles chose their castles' locations very carefully. They often built castles on hills or cliffs, which were difficult for enemies to reach, or they built castles near rivers or lakes, which were difficult for enemies to cross. Being beside a river or lake also meant that castle residents had drinking water close by and a way to escape if enemies attacked.

In the early Middle Ages, most castles were motte and bailey castles. A motte was a hill on which a tower, called a keep, was built. At the bottom of the motte was a yard called a bailey, where much of the castle's day-to-day business took place. Motte and bailey castles were made of wood. Over time, stronger keeps were built of stone.

▲ In the bailey were workshops where armorers made chain mail and armor plates and blacksmiths made iron tools. Some servants and soldiers lived in wooden huts in the bailey, close to where they worked.

The Great Hall

Castles often looked beautiful from the outside, but they were noisy and uncomfortable inside. The main room was the Great Hall, where members of the household ate and were entertained by musicians and storytellers. Nobles also met with their knights in the Great Hall to discuss strategies for war.

▶ *The lord settled disputes among peasants in the Great Hall.*

◀ *Castles in the Middle Ages had simple plumbing. Holes were built into the outer walls and drained into a large pit or moat. When soldiers attacked Chateau Gaillard, in France, in 1204, some of them crawled through a plumbing hole to get inside.*

Keeping Safe

Castles had many features that protected the people inside. A castle's stone walls were thick and difficult to knock down. Some castles, called concentric castles, were surrounded by several walls. The extra walls provided better protection against invaders.

Many castle walls were crenellated at the top, which means they had parts that stuck up like teeth. Archers hid behind the higher parts, called merlons, and shot arrows through the openings, called crenels. Archers also fired arrows through arrowloops, which were narrow slits or cross-shaped openings in the wall.

Machicolations were parts of walls that stuck out farther than the rest. Soldiers dropped boiling water or rocks on attackers through holes, called murder holes, in the machicolations' floor. Sometimes, the lower sections of a castle's walls had an outward slope, called a talus, so the rocks bounced off toward the enemy.

▼ *Soldiers at Peñafiel Castle in Spain attacked enemies from both sides by shooting arrows through the arrowloops in the walls.*

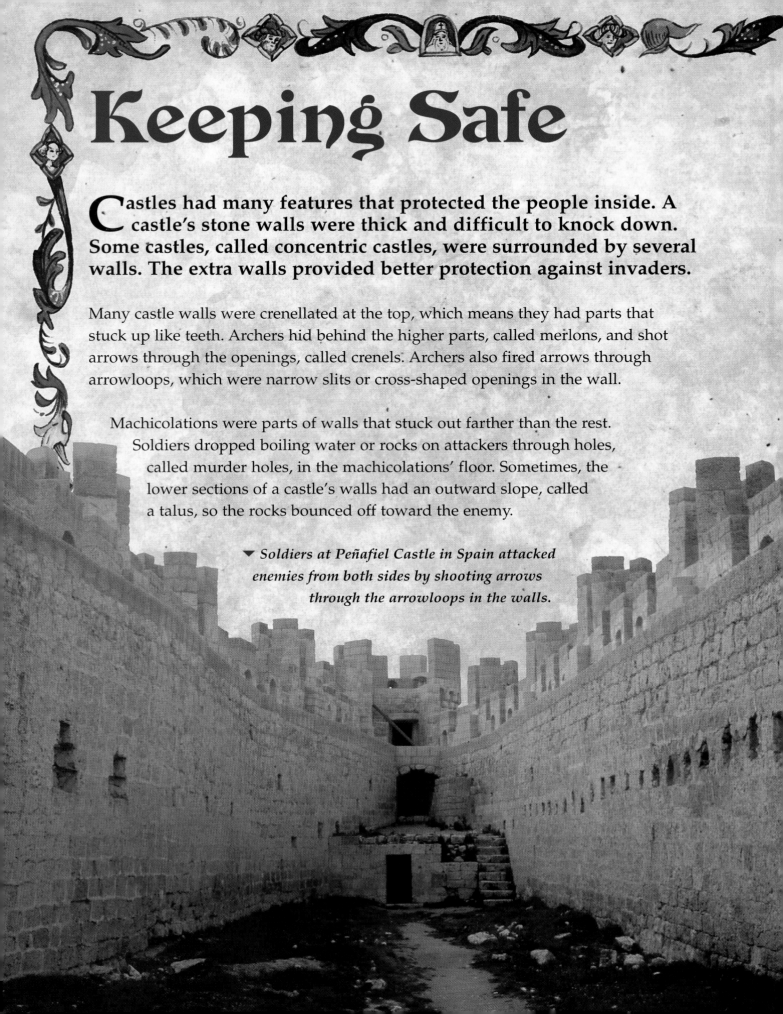

Enter if you dare!

The castle's main entrance was through a gatehouse. In front of the gate was a heavy iron fence, called a portcullis, which defenders lowered with chains and pulleys when they were under attack. Towers on either side protected the gatehouse. Stairways in the towers always curved to the right so that knights coming down the stairs had room to swing their swords.

Some castles were surrounded by a moat. This deep ditch was often filled with water. A drawbridge across the moat led to the gatehouse. In times of war, defenders pulled up the drawbridge to close off the entrance.

▶ *Water and two towers protected the gatehouse at Caerlaverock Castle, in Scotland. Enemies crossing the narrow walkway, which was rebuilt in modern times, were easy targets for castle archers.*

Siege!

During a siege, attackers continually pounded the castle with battering rams, mangonels, trebuchets, siege towers, and other weapons. The castle residents defended themselves any way they could.

Crossbows and longbows are fired through arrowloops.

Castle guards hide behind merlons.

The guard uses a forked stick to push away a scaling ladder.

Rocks bounce off the talus.

Soldiers use a scaling ladder to climb the wall.

Sappers dig a tunnel under the castle wall to make it collapse.

Wet animal skins on the roof prevent fire from spreading.

A siege tower is wheeled into position, so soldiers can leap onto the top of the castle's walls.

Everyone helps out. A castle cook pours boiling water through a murder hole in the gate tower.

The portcullis is lowered.

The drawbridge is raised.

Mattresses in front of the gate block the battering ram.

Iron caltrops are scattered on the ground to wound horses.

The trebuchet is loaded with heavy rocks.

Attackers shoot flaming arrows to set castle hoarding on fire.

Archers hide behind pavises.

On the Battlefield

Sieges were the most common kind of warfare in the Middle Ages, but battles were also fought on the battlefield. Field battles took place when an army landed on another country's shores or when people defending a castle attacked an invading army before it reached the castle.

Armies included knights and foot soldiers. Knights fought on horseback with swords. Foot soldiers fought with spears, swords, axes, and daggers. Spears were especially common because they were easy to make and use. Some spears were light enough to throw, while heavier spears were used to stab the enemy.

▼ *In the early Middle Ages, knights used wide, flat swords to slash at their enemies. These heavy swords cut through chain mail. When plate armor replaced chain mail, knights used lighter, pointy swords to stab at the spaces between the plates.*

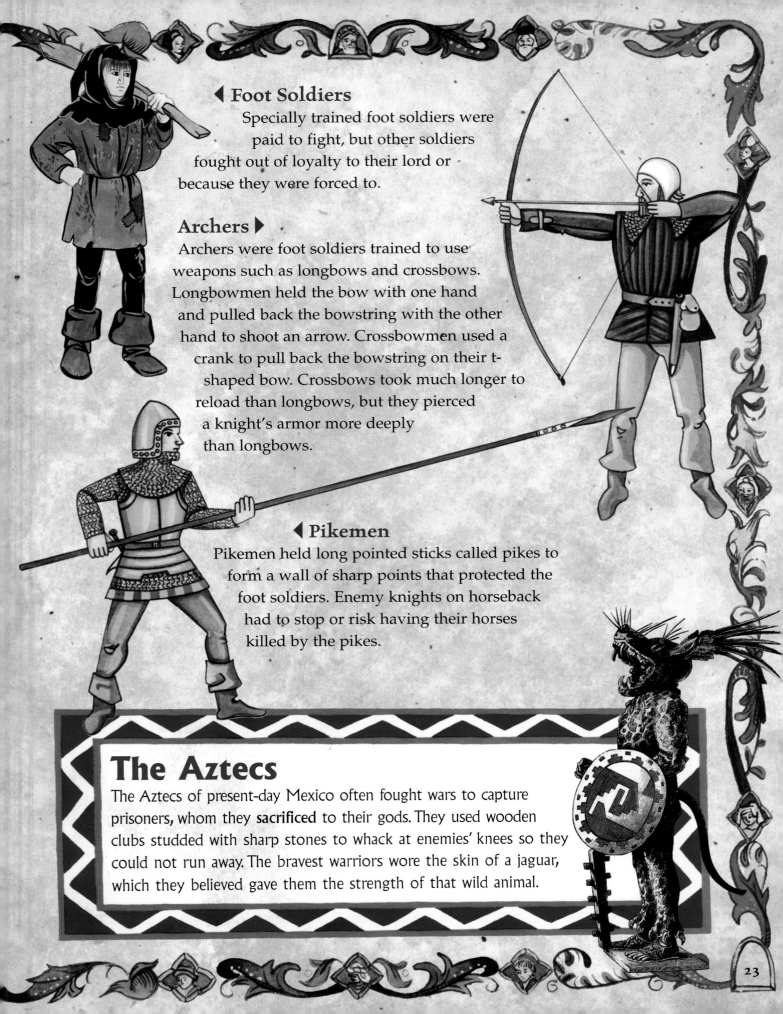

◀ Foot Soldiers

Specially trained foot soldiers were paid to fight, but other soldiers fought out of loyalty to their lord or because they were forced to.

Archers ▶

Archers were foot soldiers trained to use weapons such as longbows and crossbows. Longbowmen held the bow with one hand and pulled back the bowstring with the other hand to shoot an arrow. Crossbowmen used a crank to pull back the bowstring on their t-shaped bow. Crossbows took much longer to reload than longbows, but they pierced a knight's armor more deeply than longbows.

◀ Pikemen

Pikemen held long pointed sticks called pikes to form a wall of sharp points that protected the foot soldiers. Enemy knights on horseback had to stop or risk having their horses killed by the pikes.

The Aztecs

The Aztecs of present-day Mexico often fought wars to capture prisoners, whom they **sacrificed** to their gods. They used wooden clubs studded with sharp stones to whack at enemies' knees so they could not run away. The bravest warriors wore the skin of a jaguar, which they believed gave them the strength of that wild animal.

Famous Battles

Many important battles took place during the Middle Ages. In 1066, the winner of the Battle of Hastings became king of England. At the Battle of Courtrai, which was also known as the Battle of the Golden Spurs, foot soldiers in Belgium defeated powerful French knights, making knights less important in battles.

The Battle of Hastings

When King Edward of England died in 1066, his brother-in-law, Harold, became king. Soon, he was under attack by the Viking king Harald the Ruthless. William of Normandy, who ruled an area in present-day France, also wanted to be king of Harold's England.

Harold defeated the king of Norway in a battle in northeastern England. Right after, he and his army marched to the south of England, to Hastings, where William had landed with about 600 ships full of Norman soldiers.

On October 14, William's archers fired thousands of arrows at Harold's troops, but they were protected by a wall of shields. Soon, the archers ran out of arrows. William ordered his men to retreat, but this was just a trick. When Harold's men ran down the hill after the Normans, the Normans turned around and fought back. The English no longer had a wall of shields to protect them, and they were easily defeated. Harold was killed, and William, who became known as William the Conqueror, became the king of England.

▲ *The Bayeux Tapestry is a piece of embroidered fabric that is more than 230 feet (70 meters) long. It has 72 scenes and captions that tell the story of William's victory at the Battle of Hastings.*

▶ *The Flemish army at the Battle of the Golden Spurs fought with pikes and goedendags. These wooden clubs had iron spikes at one end, and were used to hit enemies over the head or stab them.*

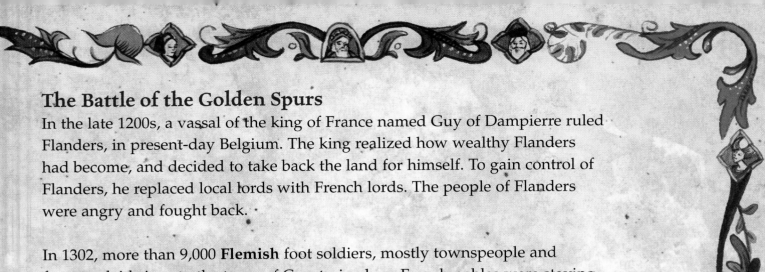

The Battle of the Golden Spurs

In the late 1200s, a vassal of the king of France named Guy of Dampierre ruled Flanders, in present-day Belgium. The king realized how wealthy Flanders had become, and decided to take back the land for himself. To gain control of Flanders, he replaced local lords with French lords. The people of Flanders were angry and fought back.

In 1302, more than 9,000 **Flemish** foot soldiers, mostly townspeople and farmers, laid siege to the town of Courtrai, where French nobles were staying. The Flemish soldiers stood in eight rows, with their pikes firmly planted in the earth. There was a river behind them and marshy land in front of them.

The powerful French army stormed the Flemish fighters, but their horses got stuck in the mud and became impaled on the pikes. The battle lasted just more than three hours, and 60 French lords and hundreds of knights were killed. This was the first battle where foot soldiers defeated an army of knights on horseback. The next day, the Flemish townspeople collected more than 500 pairs of golden **spurs** from the dead knights on the battlefield.

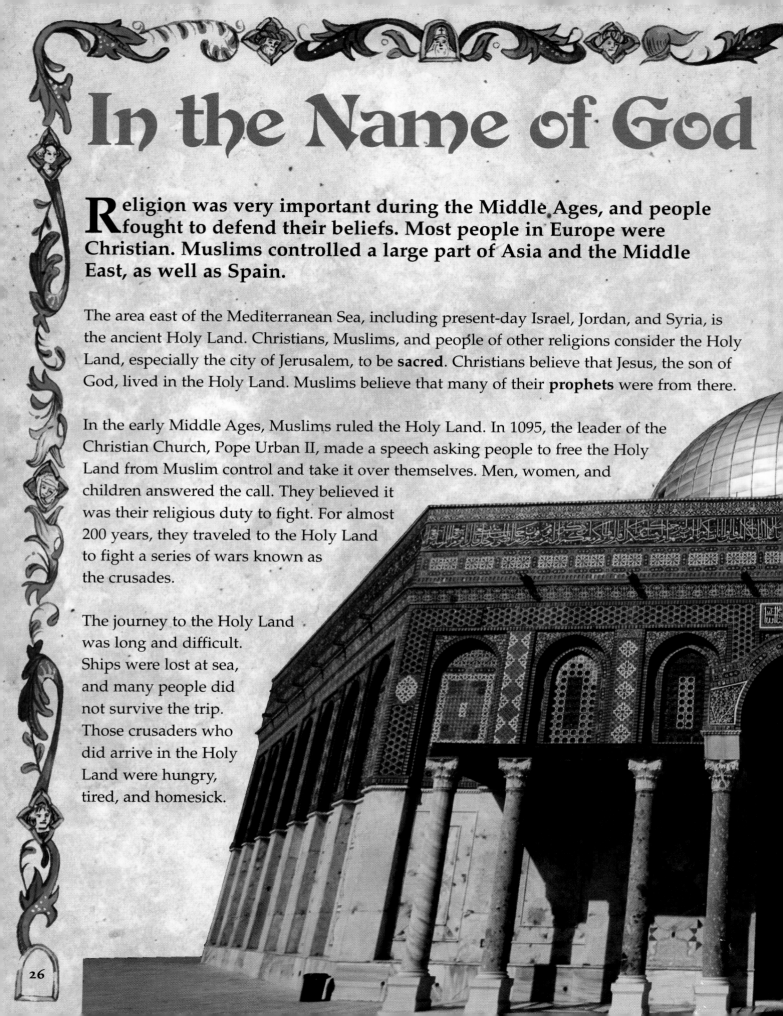

In the Name of God

Religion was very important during the Middle Ages, and people fought to defend their beliefs. Most people in Europe were Christian. Muslims controlled a large part of Asia and the Middle East, as well as Spain.

The area east of the Mediterranean Sea, including present-day Israel, Jordan, and Syria, is the ancient Holy Land. Christians, Muslims, and people of other religions consider the Holy Land, especially the city of Jerusalem, to be **sacred**. Christians believe that Jesus, the son of God, lived in the Holy Land. Muslims believe that many of their **prophets** were from there.

In the early Middle Ages, Muslims ruled the Holy Land. In 1095, the leader of the Christian Church, Pope Urban II, made a speech asking people to free the Holy Land from Muslim control and take it over themselves. Men, women, and children answered the call. They believed it was their religious duty to fight. For almost 200 years, they traveled to the Holy Land to fight a series of wars known as the crusades.

The journey to the Holy Land was long and difficult. Ships were lost at sea, and many people did not survive the trip. Those crusaders who did arrive in the Holy Land were hungry, tired, and homesick.

The People's Crusade

It took several months for Christian armies to organize the First Crusade. In the meantime, peasants from France and Germany set out to capture the Holy Land from the Muslims and keep it for themselves. A man called Peter the Hermit led the peasants on the People's Crusade. With no food or money, the members of the People's Crusade begged and stole along the way. Many of these crusaders died of hunger. Those who reached the Holy Land were killed by Muslim soldiers.

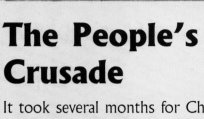

Muslims believe that Muhammad, the founder of Islam, rose to heaven from a rock that is now inside the Dome of the Rock. The Dome of the Rock is a mosque in Jerusalem that was built in the late 600s.

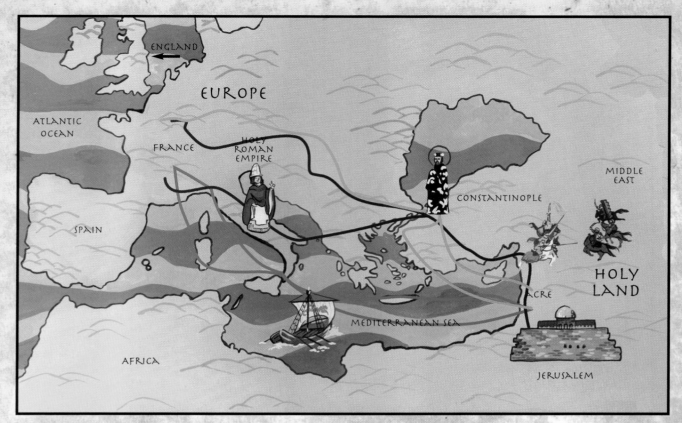

The map labels: ENGLAND, EUROPE, ATLANTIC OCEAN, FRANCE, HOLY ROMAN EMPIRE, SPAIN, CONSTANTINOPLE, MIDDLE EAST, HOLY LAND, ACRE, MEDITERRANEAN SEA, AFRICA, JERUSALEM

The Crusades

The First Crusade began in 1096. Nobles and their armies from across Europe met west of the Holy Land and took several cities by siege. Then, in 1099, more than 1,000 Christian knights and 10,000 foot soldiers attacked Jerusalem. They climbed over the city walls using siege towers and killed almost everyone they found.

The Second Crusade

After capturing Jerusalem, the leaders of the crusades set up states in the Holy Land. In 1144, the kings of France and Germany sent armies to protect the states from Muslim attacks. The armies were attacked on their way to the Holy Land, and many crusaders died of hunger and cold.

The weakened Christian troops tried to take the Muslim-held city of Damascus, north of Jerusalem, by siege. They failed. More than 10,000 crusaders were killed. Most of the others returned home.

▲ The route of the First Crusade is shown by a blue line, the Second by orange, and the Third by green.

▶ After crusaders conquered Jerusalem in the First Crusade, they thanked God for their victory. They were less successful in the seven other main crusades. The crusades ended in 1291 when the Muslims took over the last Christian state.

Muslim Society

During the time of the crusades, most people in western Europe worked as farmers or craftspeople, and few people knew how to read or write. In the Muslim world, many people lived in large cities that had universities and libraries. They were well educated in medicine, literature, **architecture**, and art. Christians returning to Europe from the crusades brought many ideas they learned from the Muslims home with them.

The Third Crusade

For a while, the Christian states in the Holy Land survived because Muslim leaders were fighting one another instead of the Christians. By 1183, the Muslims united under a powerful ruler named Saladin. Saladin recaptured Jerusalem and most of the Holy Land.

King Richard I of England, also known as Richard the Lionheart, and King Philip of France led the Third Crusade against Saladin and his army. After several battles and sieges, Richard and Saladin signed a peace agreement, which lasted five years. The treaty gave each leader territory in the Holy Land.

A New Age Begins

The Middle Ages lasted until about 1500. By that time, the feudal system was weak and the way people fought wars was changing. Europeans began to look for new ways to increase their wealth and power, rather than fighting one another for land.

The End of Knights

By the 1300s, there were fewer knights to fight. Thousands of knights had died during the crusades. Many others had sold their land before they left for the crusades to raise money for the expensive trip. Since they did not own land when they returned, they did not owe anyone military service.

During the 1350s, a disease known as the Black Plague killed almost half of Europe's population. Even fewer knights were left to fight.

Most of the remaining knights were tired of fighting. They wanted to spend their time managing their lands and enjoying their wealth. Many knights gave their lords money instead of fighting. Lords used the money to hire mercenaries.

▲ *Victims of the Black Plague were covered in large sores and usually died within days of catching the disease.*

Mercenaries were professional warriors who fought for the nobles who paid them the most. They fought for as long as they were needed, which toward the end of the Middle Ages was sometimes months or even years.

New Weapons

New weapons changed warfare. The first cannon and handguns were used in Europe in the early 1300s, but they often exploded as they were fired, missed their targets, and killed the people who shot them. After about a hundred years, guns and cannon became safer to operate and more accurate. They replaced swords, spears, bows, and arrows in wars.

▼ *Early cannon were made of copper or iron and sat on the ground supported by wood frames. The first handguns were like small cannon with long wooden handles that soldiers held under their arms.*

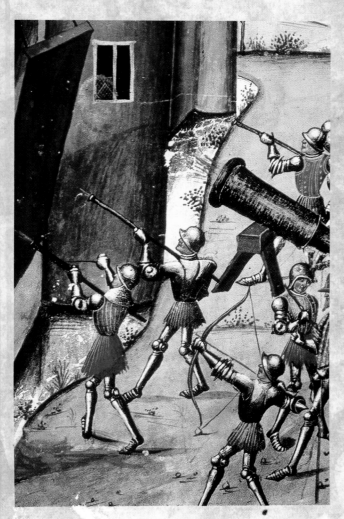

Exploration

Toward the end of the Middle Ages, rulers began to increase their wealth by sending explorers, such as Christopher Columbus, to faraway lands in search of riches. With this new age of exploration, the era of knights and castles known as the Middle Ages came to an end.

▲ *King Ferdinand and Queen Isabella of Spain sent Christopher Columbus to find a new sailing route to India. He landed in America in 1492.*

Glossary

afterlife The belief some cultures have that there is another life after death

ally A person who helps another person, especially during a war

aqueduct A structure that brings water to a town from far away

architecture The design and construction of buildings

battering ram A large weapon used to bash in castle gates

Christian A person who follows the religion of Christianity. Christians believe in one God and follow the teachings of his son on earth, Jesus Christ

empire A group of countries or territories under one ruler or government

Flemish Describing the people of Belgium

garrison Soldiers who live permanently in a castle to defend it

invader A person who enters using force

kingdom An area of land ruled by a king

moat A deep, wide ditch, often filled with water, that surrounded a castle for protection

monk A male member of a religious community who devotes his life to prayer and study

mosque A building in which Muslims pray

Muslim A person who believes in Islam, which is a religion based on the teachings of Allah and his prophet Muhammad

noble A member of a ruling class

overlord A lord who rules over other lords

priest A person who leads Christian religious ceremonies

prophet A person believed to carry a message from God

raid To make a quick surprise attack

ransom Money paid to free a prisoner

sacred Having special religious meaning

sacrifice To offer a living thing to a god as a gift

spur A sharp piece of metal worn on the heel of a horseback rider's boots, used to prick a horse to make it go faster

Index

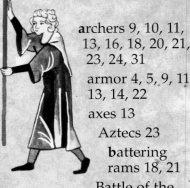

1 2 3 4 5 6 7 8 9 0 Printed in the U.S.A. 8 7 6 5 4 3